Word Sponges...

Take 5-10 minutes.

Can be student-led.

Require little or no preparation.

- Capture learner's attention.
- Turn waiting time into learning time.
- Build self-concepts.
- Create more active involvement by students.
- Stimulate creative thinking.
- Develop positive feelings for words and writing.
- Add excitement to SPELLING, READING, and LANGUAGE.

TABLE OF CONTENTS

INTRODUCTION

Word Sponges is intended for use in your classroom NOW. Both the "Table of Contents" (alphabetical listing) and the "Skills Index" are included for your convenience. Many sponges have *variations* and *extensions*. *VARIATIONS* are rule changes and ways to simplify or add complexity. *EXTENSIONS* are ways to extend into higher level thinking skills. Most sponges adapt well to a wide variety of skills and ability levels. *ARROWS* indicate more information is on the reverse side of the card.

We hope that "sponging" will spark a new interest for WORDS in your reading, spelling and language students. As you establish the "sponging" habit, you will find your students eager to repeat their favorites. Encourage them to write their own examples, clues, questions and extensions. Sponges are for everyone to create and enjoy!

Happy Sponging ...

SUGGESTIONS FOR SPONGING

Sponges:

    ... review or extend previous learning,

    ... challenge *Fast Thinkers*,

    ... focus group's attention,

    ... control crowds, and

    ... fill spare moments appropriately.

Word Sponges can take more than 5 minutes so plan accordingly. (Some *Word Sponges* extend into complete lessons in themselves.)

Although it's unnecessary, it's often helpful to prepare examples to initiate these activities. Sample ideas and lists are included to make this easier.

Sponges can be either group or individual activities. The chalkboard and overhead projector are ideal for groups; for individualized applications use paper and pencil.

SKILLS INDEX

Creative Thinking

Alphabet Messages
Crazy Compounds
Fast Lists
Guess My Word
Illustrated Idioms
Imagination
Kangaroo Words
Missing Vowels
Name Games
R-C-X

Dramatics

Conversations
Crazy Compounds
Direction Dismissal
Tune In

Letter Awareness

Disappearing Man
Letter Lists
Shapes
Who Follows Me?

Listening

Conversations
Direction Dismissal
Rhyme Time
Spell-Lleps
Spiral Spelling
Tune In

Memory

Direction Dismissal
Eraser Reading
Picture Possibilities

Oral Expression

Conversations
Guess My Word
Imagination
Rhyme Time
Shapes
Tune In
What's My Word?

Reference Skills

Blankety Blank
Dictionary Decisions
Guide Word Goal
Information Please
Kangaroo Words
Who Follows Me?

Sight Words

Eraser Reading
Flashcard Match
Lingo Bingo
What's My Word?
Word Shapes

Spelling

A to Z Lists
Blankety Blank
Crazy Compounds
Hidden Message
Kangaroo Words
Miscellaneous
Missing Vowels
Name the Same
R-C-X
Right or Wrong?
Scrambled Sentences
Spelldown
Spelling Sprint
Spell-Lleps
Spiral Spelling
Word Designs
Word Ladders
Word Shapes
Words Worth

Spelling Lists

Lingo Bingo
Spelldown
Spelling Sprint
Word Designs
Words Worth

Visualizing

Kangaroo Words
Missing Vowels
Name the Same
Scrambled Sentences
Shapes
Spell-Lleps
Spiral Spelling
Word Shapes

Vocabulary Development

A to Z Lists
Compound Chains
Crazy Compounds
Dictionary Decisions
Fast Lists
Five Square
Flashcard Match
Guess My Word
Illustrated Idioms
Letter Lists
Name Games
Rhyme Time
Selective Search
Sentence Skeletons
Ways to Say
What Belongs?
Which Doesn't Belong?
Word Ladders

Word Attack

Disappearing Man
Letter Lists
Rhyme Time
Selective Search
Syllable Spotting

Written Expression

Alphabet Messages
Basically Boring
Imagination
Name Games
Name the Same
Picture Possibilities
Right or Wrong?
Sentence Sense
Sentence Skeletons
Spiral Spelling
Telegram

Written Mechanics

Hidden Message
Scrambled Sentences

A to Z Lists

purpose: Expand vocabulary and develop fluency

prep: None

procedure: Children write the letters of the alphabet in a column down the left side of their paper. Allow 5 minutes for them to try to write a word that begins with each letter of the alphabet. Students share their responses and fill in blanks together.

suggestion: Reinforce SPELLING accuracy -- Have children use dictionaries to check their spelling.

variations: *"Category A to Z Lists"* - Write one category on the board.

> Foods   (apple to zucchini)
> Names   (Amy to Zeke)

Again the children use their A to Z column and try to
fill in as many related words as time allows.

"Oral Category A to Z Game" - Leader gives a category.
In turn students give a word for each successive letter
of the alphabet.

Vegetables
A - *asparagus*
B - *beans*
C - *corn*

"A to Z Relay" - Teams compete to fill in 2 "A to Z"
lists.

Alphabet Messages

purpose: Stimulate creative thinking
and develop sentence writing
skills

prep: None

procedure: Group brainstorms alphabet letters that can represent words
alone or in pairs, such as C, Y, or NE. Students form
short sentences using letter names.

> I C U .
>
> Y R U sad ?

Share and translate messages.

suggestion: More sentences are possible by allowing use of numbers.

> T 4 U .
>
> Is it EZ 2 write an SA ?

2

variation: Students write *"Alphabet Message Puzzles"* for class to solve.

> Which letter is a bird?
>
> Which letter is an ocean?
>
> Which letter always asks a question?

extension: Ask students to observe and share personalized license plates.

Basically Boring

purpose: Improve writing skills

prep: None

procedure: Teacher provides a simple sentence.

> Puppy barks.

Students make sentence more interesting by inserting additional word(s) for each revision.

> The cute puppy barks.
> The cute puppy barks loudly during the night.

This continues as long as possible.

suggestion: HINT -- Help students expand their sentences by posing when, where, why and how questions.

variation: Independently, students begin with a "core" sentence and go through the described elaboration steps. Students share their most expanded sentences and classmates try to determine their original "basically boring" sentence.

extension: CHALLENGE students to add <u>only</u> one word for each revision and see how far their sentence can be expanded.

> The girl jumped.
> The blonde girl jumped.
> The blonde girl jumped high.
> Quickly the blonde girl jumped high.

Blankety Blank

purpose: Apply dictionary skills and improve spelling skills

prep: None

procedure: Display words with blanks.

l _ _ p	s _ _ d
f _ _ t	g r _ _
b _ l _	_ _ m e

Children use dictionary or word list to find words that fit. Share findings.

variation: Provide beginning and ending letters only. Require 5 or more letter words.

a _____	c	p _____	t

Give special recognition for longer words.

4

"Surround It" – Give 3 letters. Students search for words that contain the 3 letters inside the word, <u>not</u> at the beginning or ending.

STI		NTR		XYG		DYB

<u>Sample Answers:</u>

a _____ c

arctic
artistic
arithmetic
athletic

sti – question
ntr – country
xyg – oxygen
dyb – ladybug

Got me Surrounded, huh?

Compound Chains

purpose: Increase awareness of compound words

prep: None

procedure: Leader selects and writes a compound word. Children use the last word of each compound as the first word for the next compound. Class attempts to make the longest possible chain of compound words.

suggestion: This is a CHALLENGING sponge.

SEE *"Crazy Compounds"* for list of compounds.

extension: CHALLENGE children to use the listed words in a meaningful paragraph or incorporate as many of the words as possible in one illustration.

Conversations

purpose: Develop oral expression skills

prep: NEED: 2 toy telephones

procedure: Select two children to conduct a telephone conversation. Teacher provides topic and "sets the stage."

> *"Give directions to your house."*

suggestion: Encourage children to recommend challenging topics.

variation: Eliminate telephone props and conduct person-to-person conversations.

> Interview a new babysitter.
> Introduce a new friend to your mother.

extension: CHALLENGE students to give accurate directions to a classmate.

> Direct another to ...
>
> tie shoes.
>
> put on a sweater.
>
> make a peanut butter sandwich.

Topic Possibilities:

Order a pizza.

Schedule a dentist appointment.

Sell a product.

Apologize for a mistake.

Report a missing person.

Call for a weather report.

Describe a new purchase.

Register a complaint.

Crazy Compounds

purpose: Increase awareness of compound words

prep: None

procedure: Each student thinks of a compound word to illustrate or act out. Students share their *"crazy compounds"* and class tries to identify the compound word.

suggestion: Reinforce SPELLING -- Each guess must also include the correct spelling.

variation: Have class search and list compound words that lend themselves to unique and humorous interpretations.

extension: Children create new compound words to illustrate the meaning of common words.

```
clock   = timeteller
window  = outsideviewer
ski     = snowslider
teacher = questionasker
```

List of Compounds:

airmail	grasshopper	newsstand	suitcase
arrowhead	gumdrop	nightfall	tiptoe
bulldozer	headdress	outdoors	toadstool
butterfly	horseshoe	pancake	treehouse
cowboy	icebox	paperback	understand
cupcake	jumprope	quarterback	wallpaper
doorman	junkyard	quicksand	waterfall
eggplant	lawnmower	raindrop	weekend
eyeglass	lifesaver	rattlesnake	wildlife
fishhook	meatloaf	shoehorn	yardstick
football	milkshake	starfish	zookeeper

Dictionary Decisions

purpose: Increase vocabulary and apply
                  dictionary skills

prep: NEED: Dictionary for each student

                  Prepare specific questions.

procedure: Students respond "yes" or "no" <u>and</u>
                  <u>why</u> to the teacher's question.

> Would you have an *oculist* check your ears?
>
> Does Mork have *charisma*?
>
> Are you subtracting when you *enumerate*?

Next students check their answers with a dictionary and
write a sentence using the new word correctly.

suggestion: Try one a day to build vocabulary and develop a weekly list
                  of new words.

Encourage students to create
questions for the class.

Additional Examples:

Do you *transcribe* at school?

Does our class feel *zealous*
about P.E.?

Would you want a teacher to
prate?

Would you want your report to
be *superlative*?

Do you enjoy being *reprimanded*?

Is Smiley a *misnomer* for a
grumpy person?

Should a *facetious* remark be
taken seriously?

Is it helpful to act *cantankerous*?

Is it polite to
masticate your food?

Direction Dismissal

purpose: Improve listening and memory skills

prep: None

procedure: Leader gives 3 or more directions.

> Hop 3 times.
> Touch your left foot.
> Turn around twice.

Students follow the directions. Teacher dismisses some children before giving another 3 or 4 part direction. Procedure continues until all students are dismissed.

variation: *"Dismissal Drawing"* - Each student draws a picture following the leader's directions. Drawing is each child's ticket to recess.

> Draw a large square in the middle.
> Make a tree left of the square.
> Draw a circle in the right top corner.
> Make your square into a house.

extension:

Stimulate IMAGINATION -- Give directions that require students to pantomine.

```
Put a saddle on a horse.
Mount your horse.
Grab the reins.
Try to make him go.
```

More Examples:

```
Buy an ice cream cone.
Begin eating it.
The top scoop begins to fall.
Try to save your cone.
```

```
Watch an exciting television show.
The TV set stops working.
Try to fix it.
Act out what happens next.
```

Disappearing Man

purpose: Practice word attack skills

prep: Draw a similar geometric man on the board. Fill in body parts with the letter sounds to be practiced.

procedure: Leader gives word. Each child responds with the correct sound *and letter*; then erases the body part that contains that letter. Activity continues until man disappears.

suggestion: Allow adequate time for man to disappear. This is an *ideal* dismissal sponge.

variation: Ask students to name and erase the body part that has a WORD that:

> rhymes with dad
> has 2 silent letters
> means the opposite of hot

Play *"Disappearing Firetruck"*
or *"Disappearing Schoolhouse."*

Reinforce SYLLABICATION skills --
Fill body parts with 2's, 3's,
4's and 5's. Leader gives word
and child responds with correct
number of syllables.

extension: With either letters or words,
require students to provide
clues in order for classmates
to respond and erase.

Eraser Reading

purpose: Practice recognition of sight words.

prep: Write words on the board.

procedure: Leader calls out a word. Student finds the word, uses it in a sentence and erases it.

suggestion: This is an *ideal* dismissal sponge for young readers.

variations: GROUP Practice -- Teacher erases a word, then group says erased word. As group gains confidence, teacher increases the number of words erased and group must state words in the order that they were erased.

Use *"Eraser Reading"* procedure with sentence pocket chart filled with flashcards. Teacher removes 2 or 3 cards and children recite removed words.

Fast Lists

purpose: Develop fluency and stimulate creative thinking

prep: None

procedure: Allow 3 to 5 minutes for students to make a list of words related to the given category.

> C I R C U S

Share and compare lists.

suggestion: Keep *"Fast Lists"* to use for future writing activities.

variation: Reinforce SPECIFIC SKILLS by having students list words related to day's lesson. List words that

> ... start with ___

... rhyme with _____

... end in _____

... mean the same as _____

... describe a _____ (beach, pirate, old person).

Ideas for Additional Lists:

Action Words
Associated Pairs
Beach Words
Book Titles

Cooking Words
Feeling Words
Foods
Health Words

Holiday Words
Home Words
Indians
Insects

Musical Words
Opposites
Propaganda Words
Rhyming Words

School Words
Shopping Words
Size Words
Special Interests

Teenage Words
Tired Words
Words with Apostrophes
Words with Multiple Meanings

Five Square

purpose: Build vocabulary and practice categorizing

prep: Draw a 5 by 5 grid on board. A 5 letter word goes across the top and the left side is labeled with categories.

procedure: Children contribute items that begin with the above letters and fit the listed categories. Each item is written in its proper square. Group attempts to see how many of the 25 squares they can fill.

suggestion: Avoid words with many vowels or repeating letters for the heading.

variation: SIMPLIFY -- Use 3 or 4 letter words with 3 or 4 categories.

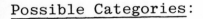

Possible Categories:

Animals	Mammals
Books	Nouns
Boys' Names	Places
Cars	Plants
Cities	Sports
Colors	States
Famous People	TV Programs
Foods	Verbs
Girls' Names	2-syllable Words

Flashcard Match

purpose: Practice sight words and increase vocabulary

prep: NEED: Flashcard set for each child

procedure: Flashcards are displayed on each child's desk. Leader gives clues about one of the words.

> You read a _____ .

Flashcard is turned face down when word is identified. The procedure continues until only one flashcard remains. Then roles reverse and students give leader clues about the remaining word.

Other Word Flashcard Activities:

Pairs play *"Concentration"* with two sets of flashcards.

Small groups play *"Rummy"* or *"Fish"* with several sets of flashcards.

Students illustrate flashcards.

Guess My Word

purpose: Expand vocabulary

prep: None

procedure: Leader thinks of a word. Students try to identify the word by asking questions that can be answered by "yes" or "no," similar to *"Twenty Questions."* Each question posed is tallied until 20 questions have been asked or the word is identified.

suggestion: Record number of questions asked and try to break that record.

extension: *"Guess My Title"* - Same procedure but students try to identify familiar book or movie title.

Guide Word Goal

purpose: Practice using guide words

prep: NEED: 2 different word lists
                         on chalkboard
                     Dictionary for each team

procedure: Select two teams for a relay
race.   In turn, each team
member goes to the dictionary,
locates the word, and writes
guide words on either side of
the listed word.   Relay teams
receive points for accuracy, correct spelling and speed.

suggestion: Include words that are also guide words.

variation: SIMPLIFY -- Every child has their own dictionary.   Teacher
calls out a word and children locate word and write its
guide words.

Hidden Message

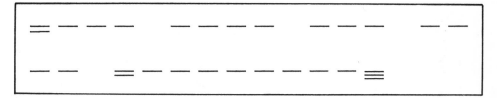

purpose: Improve spelling, punctuation and capitalization skills

prep: None

If desired, plan message.

procedure: Leader writes a message on the chalkboard using lines and spaces.
(2 lines indicate capital letters and 3 lines indicate punctuation marks.)

Format is like *"Hangman."* Children take turns guessing letters as leader fills in the message.

suggestion: This sponge is an *ideal* way to communicate important messages:

> Open House will be next Tuesday.
>
> Is your desk tidy?

variation: *"Hangman"* (single words) is a popular sponge that reinforces spelling skills and can easily be led by students.

Answer to Example:

What will you be on Halloween?

Illustrated Idioms

purpose: Increase awareness of figurative language

prep: None

procedure: Teacher provides examples of idioms.

> I have my eye on you.
>
> Mom is tied up at the office.
>
> Dad is playing bridge.

Children select one idiom to illustrate and share with the class. Class tries to identify illustrated idiom. Conclude with a discussion of both the literal and figurative meanings.

suggestion: HINT -- *"Mork and Mindy"* is an excellent resource for examples of idioms.

18

variation: Integrate DRAMATICS -- Have small groups plan and dramatize idioms for the class to guess.

List of Idioms

all thumbs	jumped out of my skin
blew her stack	lend me a hand
blew the test	nose buried in a book
cracks me up	on pins and needles
cut corners	open a can of worms
driving me crazy	pass time of day
end of my rope	splitting headache
gets in my hair	tickled pink
in the doghouse	trick up his sleeve

Imagination

purpose: Stimulate creative thinking and develop visualizing skills

prep: None

procedure: Leader writes word on board.

Students expand idea in their mind by making it

... *exaggerated*
... *impossible*
... *tragic*
... *fantastic*
... *ridiculous*

Children illustrate and share their favorite idea.

tree	milk	spider

Information Please

purpose: Improve research skills

prep: NEED: Reference books

Prepared questions

procedure: Teacher asks 3 questions. The students answer the questions by referring to appropriate reference books.

> How many definitions are listed for *run*?
>
> Is there another way to spell *disc*?
>
> What are the two ways to pronounce *record*?

suggestion: This sponge works well with SCIENCE or SOCIAL STUDIES textbooks. Prepared questions require children to skim for specific information.

variation: Use ALMANACS or the <u>Guinness Book of World Records</u>.   Ask
questions like:

How high is the highest mountain in the world?

What is the largest desert in the world?

Name the two longest rivers in the world.

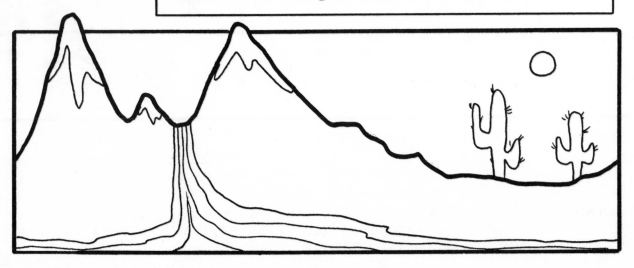

Kangaroo Words

purpose: Increase awareness of words and improve spelling skills

prep: None

procedure: Class searches for words which contain smaller words.

> escape = cap, ape
>
> together = to, the, her
>
> blossom = loss

suggestion: Increase PARTICIPATION -- Instead of immediately sharing smaller word, students give clues about their smaller word.

variation: INCREASE DIFFICULTY -- Allow students to omit letters when searching for *"Kangaroo Words."*

```
thought      =   hug, hot, out
beautiful    =   bet, eat, but
```

extension: CHALLENGE students to find a word that contains a smaller word that is a SYNONYM for itself.

```
SEPARATE   =   part
OBSERVE    =   see
SALVAGE    =   save
```

Letter Lists

purpose: Expand vocabulary and practice letter sounds

prep: None

procedure: On the chalkboard write a letter, such as <u>L</u>. Students think of as many words as they can that start with <u>L</u> and list them.

suggestion: Reinforce SPELLING ACCURACY by requiring correct spellings for credit.

variations: Reinforce other SOUNDS: consonant blends, specific vowel sounds (ou, ay, oi), or ending combinations (tion, ing, ent, ock, ill).

Integrate ART -- Provide a large outline of a block letter. Students fill letter with drawings that begin with that letter.

22

Lingo Bingo

procedure: Practice recognition of sight words or improve spelling skills

prep: List words on board or sheet.

purpose: Students draw a 3 by 3 grid (or *Tic Tac Toe* form with a border) and fill it with words from the list. Using the leader's clues, students identify and cross out the correct word. When a child has crossed out three words in a row, he calls out *"Lingo Bingo,"* and becomes the new leader.

suggestion: *If time allows*, continue play for more winners or until someone's board is completely covered.

variations: LONGER GAME -- Use a 5 by 5 grid.

FASTER GAME -- Each child chooses 5 of the SPELLING WORDS and lists them on paper. Leader calls out words at random until all of someone's words have been called.

Miscellaneous

purpose: Practice spelling skills

prep: None

procedure: Leader selects a long
word, like

> M I S C E L L A N E O U S.

Students use the letters in the word to form as many other
words as possible.

suggestion: HINT -- Students will enjoy more success if they place each
letter in the selected word on small pieces of paper that
can easily be rearranged.

variation: CALENDAR Application -- Select seasonal words or months.

Jan. - Resolutions	Mar. - Leprechaun
Feb. - Presidents	Apr. - Forecast

May	– Friendship	Sept.	– Education
June	– Achievement	Oct.	– Frankenstein
July	– Independence	Nov.	– Discoveries
Aug.	– Relaxation	Dec.	– Celebrations

Missing Vowels

purpose: Increase awareness of word structure and reinforce spelling skills

prep: None

procedure: Leader thinks of a word then displays it without its vowels.

t c h
g h t

Children attempt to identify the word by saying and spelling words that fit. Person who identifies the word becomes the new leader.

suggestion: When group is experienced, specify categories such as, book titles or names of places.

CHRLTT'S WB

```
SLND  F  TH  BL  DLPHN

NW   YRK

DSNLND

RKNSS
```

variation: SIMPLIFY -- Draw dashes to indicate location and number of
missing vowels.

```
B l _ c k  B _ _ _ t _
```

extension: Have students write and decode "messages" with missing
vowels.

Answers to Examples:

        Charlotte's Web
        Island of the Blue Dolphin
        New York
        Disneyland
        Arkansas

Name Games

purpose: Stimulate creative thinking and improve sentence writing skills

prep: None

procedure: Students print name vertically along the left margin. Each letter in their name begins a word or phrase that describes themself.

K *ind*
A *rtistic*
R *eliable*
E *ager*
N *oisy*

Koalas always recommend eating nuts.

variations: Use the letters in your name as the first letter of each word in a sentence.

26

Use the letters in your first and last name to see how many words you can make.

Figure the value of your name (SEE *"Words Worth"*). Order classmates' names according to their values.

Integrate ART -- Write your name in color. Trace around larger and larger with different colors to make a name design.

extension:

"Name Pyramids" - Begin with the first letter of your name. Add a letter each time and see how many words you can make.

```
            T
           t o
          t a p
         t a l k
        t a b l e
       t u r k e y
      t r o u b l e
     t e r r i b l e
```

Name the Same

purpose: Reinforce spelling skills

prep: None

procedure: Leader thinks of 2 words
that have <u>only</u> 1 letter in
common.

> cough
>
> walking

Leader says the 2 words and uses them in a sentence. The
students attempt to identify the common letter. They
respond by writing the letter in the air, on the carpet or
on a piece of paper.

suggestions: This sponge *isn't* as easy as it appears.

INTRODUCE this activity with easier 3 letter words, like
cat and tub.

extension: Find word pairs that share 2 (or 3) letters in common and use them in a single sentence.

h o l i d a y

m i s t a k e

I will not make a *mistake* by going to school on a *holiday*.

Picture Possibilities

purpose: Recognize main idea of a picture and improve writing skills

prep: NEED: Picture

procedure: Children study displayed picture. Class brainstorms descriptive words and phrases. Students share ideas for a title of the picture. Additional possibilities:

> Write 3 sentences about the picture.
>
> Write 3 questions about the picture.
>
> Write and solve a math story problem about the picture.
>
> Tell what happened before.
>
> Tell what will happen next.

variation: Improve VISUAL MEMORY -- Class studies picture for 30 seconds. Remove picture and ask questions.

R-C-X

red-xcx
the-cxc
hat-xRR
eat-RRR

purpose: Reinforce spelling skills

prep: None

procedure: Leader thinks of a 3 letter word. Students try to discover the word by saying and spelling 3 letter words. Leader responds to each suggested word with coded feedback.

> R = correctly placed letter in my word
> C = misplaced letter that's in my word
> X = letter is not in my word

Activity continues until someone discovers the word and receives feedback: *"RRR."*

suggestion: SIMPLIFY and introduce activity with 2 letter words.

INCREASE DIFFICULTY -- Extend activity to 4 letter words
when students achieve success with 3 letter words.

CHALLENGE students by listing feedback with R's followed
by C's <u>not</u> according to letter's position in the particular
word.

suit	X	X	X	X
hear	C	X	X	X
bare	R	X	X	X
fast	X	X	X	X
dogs	R	X	X	X
dent	C	X	X	X
hate	R	X	X	X
hope	R	R	X	X
vote	R	R	C	X
move	R	R	R	X
love	R	R	R	R

Rhyme Time

purpose: Increase vocabulary and develop oral expression skills

prep: None

procedure: Teacher thinks of a word and gives class a rhyming word clue.

> "My word rhymes with set."

Class tries to guess word by asking questions about rhyming words.

> "Is your word a fast airplane?"
>
> ... "No, it's not a *jet*."
>
> "Can a dog or cat be your word?"
>
> ... "No, it's not a *pet*."
>
> "Does your word mean upset?"
>
> ... "No, it's not a *fret*."

Clue questioning continues until word is identified. Together class says and spells word.

suggestion: As each clue question is asked have total class determine the rhyming word.

Right or Wrong?

purpose: Reinforce spelling skills and practice writing sentences

prep: None

procedure: Write 3 words on the board; one is misspelled. Children decide which word is wrong, and write one sentence using the two correctly spelled words. Before sharing students' sentences, correct the misspelled word.

> *school   lern   fourth*
>
> I was the <u>fourth</u> one off the <u>school</u> bus.

suggestion: Have children design sets of words with one misspelled word.

variation: INCREASE DIFFICULTY -- Use
                   sets of 4 or 5 words.

minit guess although library
haven't receive frends cousin
jealous calender delicious neighbor

Scrambled Sentences

purpose: Strengthen visual perception skills and reinforce spelling skills

prep: None

If desired, plan message and arrangement.

procedure: Leader writes sentence.

> C anyo use e them ess age ?

Students study and decode message. Discovered message is rewritten with correct arrangement of letters and spacing.

suggestion: Encourage leader to proofread his "message" for spelling, capitalization and punctuation accuracy.

variations: SIMPLIFY -- Scramble order of words within a sentence.

> chocolate like ice I cream.

32

Scramble letters within each word, maintaining proper
spacing.

| Anc uyo nifd ym geemass ? |

Selective Search

purpose: Reinforce specific word attack skills

prep: None

procedure: Select a passage in a textbook. Children search passage for words that are examples of a word attack skill being studied and list them on paper.

> Find and list two
> syllable nouns.

variation: TIMED ACTIVITY -- See how many words group can find in a specified amount of time.

extension: After students complete the task, they use their listed words to make a related list. For example, they could use their list of nouns to make plurals.

Possible *Search* Topics:

adjectives

blends (bl, cr)

compound words

contractions

double consonants

hard & soft "g" sounds

homonyms

long vowel words

opposites

rhyming words

plurals

possessives

synonyms

words with prefixes

words with silent letters

3 syllable words

Sentence Sense

purpose: Reinforce sentence writing skills

prep: None

procedure: Teacher gives class a set of 3 words.

> elephant
> mouse
> peanuts

Students use words in any order to write one meaningful and complete sentence. Share and discuss results. Continue the activity with additional 3 word sets.

suggestion: Use 3 word sets created by students.

INCREASE DIFFICULTY -- Require students to use the words
in a specified order ot give them sets of 4 or 5 words.

List of 3 Word Sets

crowd	delicious	flashing
cheering	sizzling	clown
outstanding	morsels	yellow
gigantic	mistake	mysterious
purple	tent	haunted
parade	tornado	wandering

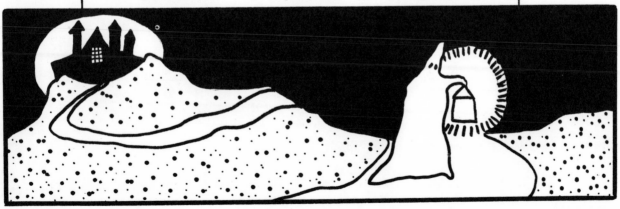

Sentence Skeletons

purpose: Improve writing skills and increase vocabulary

prep: None

procedure: Leader selects a word that can be both a noun and a verb. Word is placed in sentence skeletons on the board.

Bat ____ ____ ____ .
____ bat ____ ____ .
____ ____ bat ____ .
____ ____ ____ bat.

Children write sentences that fit the *"sentence skeletons."*

variation: INCREASE DIFFICULTY -- Use 5 or 6 word sentence skeletons

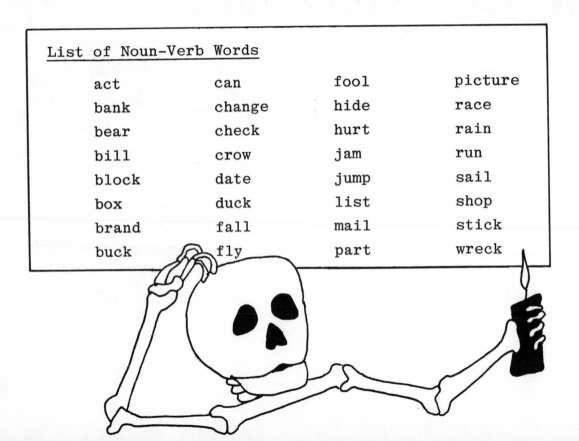

List of Noun-Verb Words

act	can	fool	picture
bank	change	hide	race
bear	check	hurt	rain
bill	crow	jam	run
block	date	jump	sail
box	duck	list	shop
brand	fall	mail	stick
buck	fly	part	wreck

Shapes

purpose: Increase awareness of letters and reinforce letter & shape recognition

prep: Draw overlapping shapes with letters.

procedure: Students use drawing to answer leader's questions.

> "Which vowel is inside the circle?"
>
> "Which letter is inside all 3 shapes?"
>
> "Which shapes contain letters that are in your name?"

OR students ask questions to locate leader's letter.

> "Is it a tall letter?"
>
> "Is it it the word 'bread'?"

INCREASE DIFFICULTY -- Add fourth overlapping shape, such as a hexagon, trapezoid, square or oval.

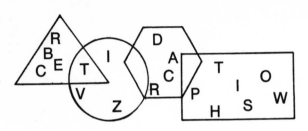

Try activity with words instead of letters.

Questions can reinforce many skills.

How many consonants are inside the triangle?

How many letter names in the triangle rhyme with tree?

Use letters inside the hexagon to spell a word.

Can you use the letters in a different shape to spell a word?

Spelldown

purpose: Reinforce spelling skills

prep: None

procedure: Each student thinks of a 4 or 5 letter word that contains no repeating letters. Students write their word on a piece of paper. As letters of the alphabet are called out, children cross them out (like *"bingo"*). When all the letters are crossed out, child spells his word and becomes the new leader.

suggestion: This is an *ideal* dismissal sponge for the end of a spelling period. Each child leaves when he has crossed out all the letters of his word.

variation: INCREASE DIFFICULTY -- Require that words have a minimum number of letters and/or syllables.

Spelling Sprint

purpose: Reinforce spelling skills

prep: NEED: Large alphabet cards

procedure: Distribute cards to students. Leader calls out a word. Students holding the required letters go to the front and arrange themselves to spell the word. Classmates indicate the word is correctly spelled by giving group the "thumbs up" signal.

Before going on to new word, have students try to rearrange themselves to spell another word.

suggestion: If less than 26 students participate, select letters that are frequently found in words.

variation: Select 4 students and see if they can form a word.

extension: TEAM GAME -- Give each team a set of mixed letters. Teams compete to discover and correctly spell a word using all the letters. *(Beforehand place letters for specific long words in envelopes.)*

Spell-Lleps

purpose: Improve perception skills and reinforce spelling skills

prep: None

procedure: Leader thinks of a word and spells it aloud BACKWARDS. Class tries to identify the word. Each child who knows the word, gives class an additional clue.

> "It's usually brown, black and white."
>
> "You use its keys."
>
> "It's an instrument."

When most students seem to know the word, total group says and spells the word.

suggestion: It's HELPFUL to repeat spelling of word between clues.

SIMPLIFY -- For younger students
spell word correctly (forwards)
using the same clue format.

Spiral Spelling

purpose: Reinforce spelling skills

prep: None

procedure: Leader writes word on the chalkboard. Chalk is then handed to a volunteer who begins his word with the last letter of the previously written word. Spiral pattern continues as chalk is handed around the group.

suggestions: This is an *ideal* dismissal sponge.

Try this activity with groups of 4. (Each group will need a large piece of drawing paper and 4 different colored pencils.)

variation: Increase VISUALIZATION and AUDITORY DISCRIMINATION SKILLS -- Play *"Spiral Spelling"* as an oral activity.

"Spiral Sentence" - Each child writes a sentence, a comma and a connective word.

> I wanted to go, but
> *my father said no, so*
> we stayed home, and

Syllable Spotting

purpose: Increase awareness of syllables

prep: None

procedure: Teacher states a category and a number over 5.

Fruit	10

Students list fruit words whose combined syllables total 10.

banana + apple + cantaloupe + orange + grapes = 10

variation: SIMPLIFY -- Have students list related words and find total number of syllables.

CHALLENGE students by having them find 3 related words and expressing them in a math equation.

```
aunts + uncles = relatives
ladder - rung   = fall
candy +  pie    = calories
```

SEE *"Five Square"* for list of categories.

Telegram

purpose: Discriminate between necessary & unnecessary words in sentences and improve writing skills

prep: Plan message.

procedure: Teacher writes a message on the board.

Reminder

Your science fair projects are <u>due</u> Wednesday, March 20th. Parents and visitors will see the exhibits on Thursday evening.

Children try to write a *"telegram"* version of the message using only as many words as necessary.

suggestion: For FUN give a "cost per word" rate and see who can write the most economical messages.

variation: For SENTENCE WRITING PRACTICE -- Provide the *"telegram"* version and have the students expand the message into sentence form.

extension: Improve COMPREHENSION SKILLS -- After students have read a story, they write a telegram summarizing it.

Tune In

purpose: Improve oral expression skills

prep: None

procedure: Select 4 or 5 children to simulate a radio program. Teacher signals when making a station change and speakers immediately alter content to fit the new program selection.

Program possibilities:

> News -- Commercial -- Opera --
> Sports Commentary -- Weather --
> Traffic Report

suggestion: Use cards to signal next program.

variation: *"T.V. Tune In"* - Require participating students to act out
as well as speak. Additional program possibilities:

Cartoons -- Game Shows -- Exercise Class --
Soap Opera -- Situation Comedy

Ways to Say

purpose: Expand vocabulary

prep: None

procedure: Select and write an overused word on the chalkboard.

says

Children list other *"ways to say"* the selected word.

suggestion: Generate MORE RESPONSES by asking, "How many ways can a person *speak*?"

variation: Use *"Modifier Rings"* to reduce the use of words like <u>really</u> and <u>very</u>.

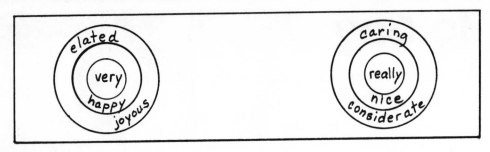

Possible Answers:

<u>says</u>	advises	declares	expresses	reveals
	asks	demands	informs	screams
	announces	discloses	orders	whispers
	communicates	divulges	recites	yells

<u>very happy</u>

blissful	ecstatic
contented	jubilant
delighted	pleased

<u>really nice</u>

agreeable	helpful
amiable	pleasant
friendly	reliable

What Belongs?

purpose: Build vocabulary and awareness of word relationships

prep: Plan sample word arrangements to get activity started.

procedure: Students study word arrangement.

letter	word
sentence	

They try to discover the relationship of the top two words and complete the missing part so the bottom words relate similarly.

variation: SIMPLIFY -- Have children add an additional word to a list of 2 or 3 related words and name the category.

car	bus	plane	_____

touch	baseball	cake	Earth
taste	soccer	pie	Mars
_____	_____	cookies	Mercury
		_____	_____

Other Examples:

city	*county*		*hand*	*finger*		*whale*	*ocean*
state			*foot*			*lizard*	

pedal	*bike*		*peacock*	*bird*		*wolf*	*wolves*
row			*bear*			*deer*	

Answers to Examples:

green	country	desert	mammal
paragraph	toe	boat	deer

What's My Word?

purpose: Practice recognition of sight words

prep: List words on a sheet for each child.

procedure: Teacher gives clues about one of the words.

> "My word is a naming word.
> It has one silent letter.
> It rhymes with fight.
> It's a toy."

As students identify the word they point to it on their sheet. When the majority of the students have identified the word, they call it out in unison.

suggestion: This is an *ideal* way to provide group practice before your children cut up a sheet of word flashcards.

Practice ORAL EXPRESSION skills -- Leader THINKS of a word from the list. Classmates ask questions to identify the leader's word.

Which Doesn't Belong?

purpose: Increase understanding of word meanings and discover word analogies

prep: None

procedure: Display arrangement of 4 words. Students study words. They try to discover how 3 of the words share something in common and identify which word doesn't belong. When they identify the "misfit," they also explain WHY.

hot	soft		Billy	Susan		train	laugh
sweet	rough		George	Steven		rose	see

suggestion: Use arrangements created by your children.

pitcher	shortstop	fresh	modern
catcher	linebacker	archaic	recent

Answers to Examples:

sweet	- others can be felt
George	- others are 2 syllables
see	- others can be verbs or nouns
linebacker	- others play baseball
archaic	- others are synonyms for new

Who Follows Me?

purpose: Improve alphabetizing skills

prep: NEED: Large alphabet cards

procedure: Cards are distributed so each child knows only his own card. One child is selected to share his letter.

> "I have <u>K</u>,
>
> who follows me?"

Student with <u>L</u> shows his card <u>and</u> chooses a classmate to begin another round. Activity continues until everyone has an opportunity to participate.

variation: Require students to say a word that begins with their letter.

Word Designs

purpose: Increase awareness of words and reinforce spelling skills

prep: NEED: Grid paper

List words on board or sheet.

procedure: Using grid paper, students arrange as many words as possible in a connecting, crossword design. Share and discuss different arrangements.

suggestion: It's fun to GRAPH the number of words successfully connected in the students' *"word designs."*

extension: *"Category Word Designs"* - Teacher provides an arranged *"word design"* grid. A category (places, toys, size words) is selected. Students fill predesigned grid with words that fit the category.

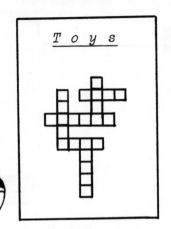

_T o y s_

List of Categories

action words	feelings	school
adjectives	foods	shopping
animals	greetings	sounds
calendar	numbers	sports
city	plants	weather

Word Ladders

purpose: Build vocabulary and reinforce spelling skills

prep: None

procedure: Leader begins by saying and writing a 4 letter word on the chalkboard.

> card

Someone forms another word by changing one letter (care, cord, cart, hard, etc.). This continues until no one can think of an additional word. Group attempts to see how far their ladders can go.

variation: *"Word Ladder Puzzles"* - Have students design 4 or 5 step ladders for class to solve.

> How many word changes does it take to get from *warm* to *cold*?

➡

Can you get from *fat* to *pig* in 3 changes?

Can you get from *card* to *post* with 4 changes?

Answers to Puzzles:

WARM	w<u>o</u>rm	wor<u>d</u>	<u>c</u>ord	COLD
FAT	f<u>i</u>t	fi<u>g</u>	PIG	
CARD	car<u>t</u>	<u>p</u>art	p<u>o</u>rt	POST

Word Shapes

purpose: Reinforce word structure for reading & spelling

prep: List words on board or sheet.

procedure: Leader draws configuration of a selected word.

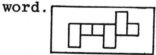

Students use configuration clue and word list to identify the word. *Fast thinkers* help class recognize word by giving meaning clues.

> "It's a place."
>
> "Elephants live there."
>
> "Monkeys live there."

variation: WITHOUT a word list -- Leader selects a word and provides
configuration clue. Class asks questions in a *"20 Questions"*
format until word is identified.

Additional Example:

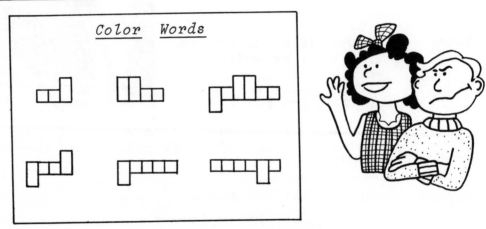

Words Worth

purpose: Reinforce spelling skills

prep: List words on board or sheet.

procedure: Each child selects and writes 5 of the listed words. Next students determine the value of their words by placing a "5" over each vowel and a "1" over each consonant. Add to find the total values.

variation: Have students order their entire SPELLING LIST according to each word's value.

extension: CHALLENGE your students by asking them to find:

"Words with high or low values."

"Words worth more than 12 but less than 20 points."

"Pairs of words with the same value."